D0687007

The Métis

JENNIFER HOWSE

Weigl

CALGARY

www.weigl.com

Published by Weigl Educational Publishers Limited
6325 10 Street SE
Calgary, Alberta, Canada
T2H 2Z9

Website: www.weigl.com

Library and Archives Canada Cataloguing in Publication Data

Howse, Jennifer
    The Métis / Jennifer Howse.

(Canadian Aboriginal art and culture)
Includes index.
ISBN 978-1-55388-337-1 (bound)
ISBN 978-1-55388-338-8 (pbk.)

    1. Métis--Juvenile literature. I. Title. II. Series.
FC109.H68 2007   j971.004'97   C2007-902196-4

Printed in the United States of America
2 3 4 5 6 7 8 9 0   11 10 09

Project Coordinator Heather Kissock   **Design** Janine Vangool   **Validator** Christi Belcourt

Photograph credits
Every reasonable effort has been made to trace ownership and to obtain permission to reprint copyright material. The publishers would be pleased to have any errors or omissions brought to their attention so that they may be corrected in subsequent printings.

Cover (top left): Courtesy of Fred Lang; **Cover (top right)**: Egon Borke/GNWT; **Cover (main):** Glenbow Archives: (AR-302-a-b); **Courtesy of Christi Belcourt:** page 27; **CP Images:** pages 1, 16, 18 top, 22, and 28; **Egon Borke/GNWT:** page 30; **Glenbow Archives:** pages 7 (NA-47-10) and 8 (PA-2218-26); **Collection of Glenbow Museum, Calgary, Canada:** 10 (AR 281), 24 (AR 215), and 25 (AR 302 a-b); **Courtesy of Fred Lang:** pages 11, 19 bottom, and 26; **Library and Archives Canada:** page 29 (PA-012854); **Mary Evans Picture Library:** page 6; **North Wind Picture Archives:** page 19.

We acknowledge the financial support of the Government of Canada through the Book Publishing Industry Development Program (BPIDP) for our publishing activities.

Please note
All of the Internet URLs given in the book were valid at the time of publication. However, due to the dynamic nature of the Internet, some addresses may have changed, or sites may have ceased to exist since publication. While the author and publisher regret any inconvenience this may cause readers, no responsibility for any such changes can be accepted by either the author or the publisher.

CONTENTS

The People

In the Canadian Constitution, **Aboriginal Peoples** are listed in three groups—**First Nations**, Inuit, and Métis. The Métis are one of the Aboriginal Peoples in Canada. There are more than 200,000 Métis people living in Canada today.

The Métis have a unique history. More than 400 years ago, European men travelled to the Canadian territories to work in the **fur trade**. During their time in Canada, they began families with First Nations women. The children of these European and First Nations unions are called Métis. These children grew up and married other Métis, and a unique culture began. Métis communities developed along fur-trade routes and near large fur-trade forts.

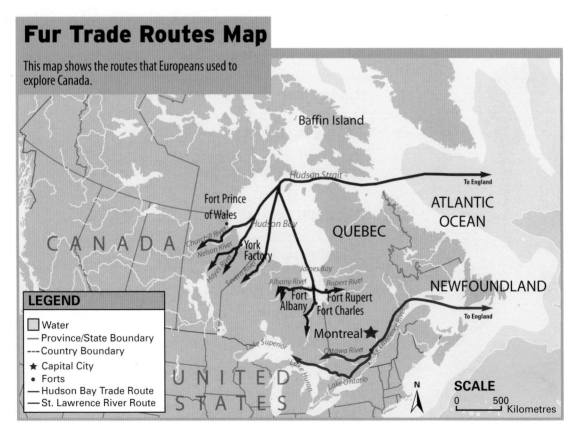

Fur Trade Routes Map

This map shows the routes that Europeans used to explore Canada.

Historically, most Métis worked in the fur trade. They also hunted bison, farmed, and transported goods. The Métis had knowledge from both sides of their families. They often had European knowledge of money, trade, and the French or English language. Métis children also learned the Cree or Ojibwa languages and received **traditional** knowledge of how to hunt and live off the land from their First Nations relatives.

The name Métis is a French term meaning "mixed." At first, the name was used for children who had French- and Cree-speaking parents. Now, the name Métis is used by people who identify themselves as having both First Nations and European **ancestors**.

The beaver was the most important animal to the fur trade. Beaver pelts were sold to Europe to make fashionable clothing and hats.

Métis Homes

Canadian winters are known for their icy temperatures. During the time of the fur trade, there was no central heating or electricity to create warmth. To protect themselves from the cold, the Métis built strong houses out of logs and sod. These homes were warmed by a fireplace made from clay and hay. These materials helped the people inside stay cozy and dry.

The log houses were constructed by first creating a wooden frame. Wood was gathered from pine trees and was then peeled and dried. The logs were cut to fit one on top of the other like a puzzle. The roof was made of layers of split logs which were covered with wood shingles or sod. Gaps in the log walls were filled with a mud and prairie-grass mixture. This prevented moisture and cold from leaking inside. Windows did not have glass. Instead, deer hides were stretched and scraped thin enough for sunlight to shine through.

Métis log homes were more permanent than traditional aboriginal homes, such as wigwams. They could not be moved quickly and easily like these other shelter

The inside of the log house had rafters, which are narrow logs that have been cut into poles. Drying animal hides and cloth slings for storing food were hung from the poles. The floor was made mostly of wood. Near the fireplace, however, the floor was covered in clay to prevent ashes from catching fire. Beds were made from wooden frames that had leather strips criss-crossing from one side to the other. These strips supported the rabbit skins or bison robes that the Métis slept on. Furniture, such as tables and chairs, was made of wood and animal hides. Pots and kettles were made of metal. Birchbark containers were used to store food.

Métis houses could have more than one family living in them.

Métis families travelled many times during the year. During their travels, they slept in **teepees**. The teepees provided a strong shelter while transporting goods or hunting bison.

Métis Communities

Most Métis communities formed because of the fur trade. Métis men performed many jobs in the fur trade, including guide, **factor**, labourer, and **voyageur**. They worked for one of the two main fur-trade companies, which were the Hudson's Bay Company and the North West Company. The Hudson's Bay Company and the North West Company set up trading posts across the country. As the Métis populations grew, Métis peoples formed settlements near the posts.

Métis trappers played an important role in the development of the fur trade.

The Red River Settlement in Manitoba and the Victoria Settlement in Alberta were well-known early Métis communities. Both settlements had European beginnings as fur-trading posts or **missions**. Both attracted Métis settlers as well. The communities were based on a mixture of farming, bison hunting, and trading.

Today, the Métis live in cities and in small rural towns throughout Canada. They work in many occupations. Métis governments provide support and encouragement for their members to start their own businesses. Many Métis now own and operate a wide range of businesses in areas such as transportation, retail, and the music industry.

The Métis National Council governs all the Métis in Canada. The provinces of Ontario, Manitoba, Saskatchewan, Alberta, and British Columbia have local councils. All of the nations are led by elected leaders. Each of these nations has a constitution. This is a set of rules that they obey. Each nation also tries to include people with different backgrounds and experiences in the council to ensure that many voices have a say in how the nation is governed.

The area now known as Winnipeg was once part of the Red River Settlement.

Métis Clothing

Traditionally, almost all of the clothing worn by the Métis was made by Métis women. Women prepared deerskins or moosehides for stitching and shaping into coats, leggings, and hats. Varieties of fabric were also available from trading posts, and Métis women incorporated these fabrics into their sewing. Sometimes, the Métis purchased and wore ready-made European clothes as well, but it was more **economical** to make the clothing from scratch. The mixing of Aboriginal and European clothing made for colourful and unique outfits.

Métis clothing could be made with traditional fabrics, such as elk skin, as well as European materials, such as velvet and cotton.

Métis women were skilled at working with European-made wool or cotton cloth. They used these materials to sew trousers and shirts for men and boys. The trousers were held up by colourfully beaded suspenders. Métis women also used Hudson's Bay Company **point blankets** to make coats called capotes. Special gear, such as snowshoes, pouches, **moccasins**, and jackets, was constructed by Métis women as well. These women created their own businesses by selling these items to fur traders.

Métis women combined European and traditional clothing to create their own unique style. The European fashion of long skirts and blouses for women was blended with Métis-style velvet or woollen leggings and shawls. These layers of clothing helped keep women warm when the weather turned cold. The Métis relied on furs to keep them warm as well. Footwear included woollen stockings worn under moosehide moccasins.

The Red River sash, or *l'Assomption*, is a finger-woven wool sash that can be up to 3 metres long. The sash can be used as a belt, a rope, a bandage for injuries, or to wrap a broken bone. It can also be used as a chain or sling to help carry heavy loads.

The sash is red, with bright yellows, greens, and blues woven into the wool. Voyageurs adorned themselves with this sash. After the fur-trade era, Métis men continued to wear the sash as a useful article of clothing. Historically, the sash was never worn by Métis women, as they wore a different style of belt that was adorned with beadwork. Today, however, the sash is worn by men, women, and children as a symbol of Métis **heritage**.

The l'Assomption sash was named after the town of Assomption in Quebec. This is where many of the first sashes were made.

Métis Food

Métis food was a mixture of First Nations and European influences. Hunting for game such as geese, deer, moose, and bison was necessary to ensure there was enough meat for families to survive long winters. Fishing was also an important food source. A long time ago, extra meat and hides were sold, and the money earned was used to buy European flour and sugar. Flour was blended with bison grease and then fried to create bannock. This bread was served with meat and vegetables, sometimes mixed together in a stew. Aside from flour and sugar, almost every other food source came from the land.

For Métis living on the Prairies, bison was the main food source. It was often used to make pemmican. Pemmican was made from bison meat that had been dried in the sunlight. Once dried, the meat was pounded into a powder and mixed with bison fat and berries. The mixture was sewn into bags and stored. Pemmican was a staple in Métis culture as it could last for years and was easy to carry when travelling.

In the 1800s, at least 30 million bison roamed North America.

In the summer months, Métis families kept vegetable gardens and picked berries from bushes that grew nearby. The berries and vegetables were often preserved for use in the winter months. Tea was another tradition that was enjoyed by the Métis, who kept water hot and ready for visitors.

Blueberries were one type of berry that could be used to make pemmican. Chokecherries, raspberries, and saskatoon berries could also be used.

Pemmican

Ingredients

1 kilogram of dried bison or beef jerky

100 millilitres of dried berries (blueberries or saskatoons)

25 millilitres animal fat

Equipment

kitchen mallet

cutting board

frying pan

large mixing bowl

plastic bags

1. Put the dried meat on the cutting board, and pound it until it flakes.

2. Melt the fat in a frying pan, and then pour it into a bowl.

3. Take the dried berries and flakes of meat, and add them to the bowl. Stir the mixture until the berries and meat are completely coated in the fat.

4. Once the mixture is cooled, roll it into large balls, and store them in plastic bags. When serving, pemmican be prepared in several ways. It can be served as is, or it can be cooked. It can also be boiled with flour and water to make a soup.

Transportation

Whether by water or by land, travelling long distances was normal for the Métis. Often, waterways were used for transporting items to the trading posts. While canoes were one mode of transportation, they were not large enough to carry big shipments. To solve this problem, the Métis developed the York boat. This wooden boat had a flat bottom and was powered by up to four sets of oars. Modelled after Scottish rowboats, the York boat could carry much more cargo and was faster and easier to row than a canoe.

Red River carts were another way to transport items to and from trading posts. These carts were first developed in the Red River region of what is now Manitoba. They were made entirely from wood that was tied together with rawhides and sinew. The carts were pulled by horses or oxen.

Red River carts were very important for travelling long distances over the prairie. The wheels could be removed so that the cart could be floated over streams like a barge. They could then be refastened once the trip returned to land.

BISON HUNTING

For Métis living on the Prairies, bison provided food and clothing, items important to their survival. Hundreds of men, women, and children travelled together to hunt the bison herds twice a year. Camp was made, and the first of many meetings was held to organize the group.

The first action was to choose a leader for the camp. The leader had captains and policemen appointed to ensure the laws of fairness and safety were upheld. These rules were known to the Métis as the Laws of the Prairie.

Métis hunters rode on fast horses called buffalo runners. They approached the bison herd and stampeded it. A good hunt could fill more than 1,200 Red River carts with hides and meat.

A bison hunt involved hundreds of men, women, children, Red River carts, and horses. Some groups would travel hundreds of kilometres to hunt bison.

Métis Religion

The Métis held a variety of **spiritual** beliefs. From their First Nations family members, they learned traditional teachings about Aboriginal spirituality. These teachings involved ceremonies and beliefs about respecting the natural world and other people. European parents taught their children about their spiritual beliefs as well. French-speaking traders practised the Catholic religion. English-speaking fathers shared their Anglican, Methodist, or Presbyterian religions. The Métis meshed their Aboriginal spirituality with these **Christian** religions to create their own belief system.

Christianity still plays an important role in the lives of many Métis.

As the land became more settled, missionaries from Great Britain and France started churches in Métis settlements. The church became a gathering place and a part of the community. Missionaries held church services before the bison hunts to bless those who would be in danger during the hunt. Catholic Métis prayed to their patron, Saint Joseph. They adorned their homes with symbols of the Church, such as crucifixes and rosaries.

A crucifix is a cross. In Christian religions, it symbolizes the sacrifice of Jesus Christ.

St. Antoine de Padoue Church is located in Batoche, Saskatchewan—the site of a major conflict between the Métis and the Canadian government in the 1800s.

Churches were very important in Métis communities. Each Métis settlement had a church, which was the centre of community activity. The churches were constructed by European missionaries. They were modelled in the same style as buildings in Great Britain and France, but with local wood and materials. The walls were painted with religious stories. Painted moosehides and Métis needlework also decorated the walls.

Ceremonies and Celebrations

In the past, one of the biggest gatherings for the Métis was the bison hunt. The bison hunt provided a social gathering for friends and family to visit with each other. Traditions, such as community suppers and dancing, were practised during these gatherings.

Religious ceremonies were another reason for the Métis to join together and celebrate. Christmas was a big event during the fur-trade era. It brought Europeans, Métis, and First Nations peoples together at the forts for a huge feast and an evening of dancing. In Métis settlements, Christmas church services were held for Roman Catholic Métis. This was the most important service of the year.

Métis communities continue to hold cultural celebrations to pass on their traditions to younger generations of Métis, as well as to display these traditions to the general public.

Today, Métis communities commemorate Louis Riel Day on November 16 of each year. Louis Reil was a Métis leader who stood up for Métis rights and land claims. In 1885, he was charged with committing **treason** against the government of Canada during the **Northwest Resistance**. As punishment, Riel was hanged on this day. Ontario's Métis nation hosts a remembrance ceremony to mark this day. In Alberta, an entire week of events is organized to remember Riel. These events include a supper held for **elders** and a dinner and dance.

RENDEZVOUS

A tradition that was started in the days of the bison hunt is the rendezvous. This is a community gathering that is similar to an Aboriginal **powwow**. The rendezvous is usually held in the summer. It brings the Métis together to participate in horse racing, dance competitions, suppers, and church services.

The Rendezvous was a chance for Métis from many different places to come together. This event often lasted up to a week.

Music and Dance

Music and dance are very important forms of entertainment for the Métis. Today, the Métis attend large gatherings to celebrate their heritage with fiddle music and jigging.

When men were recruited from the Orkney Islands in Scotland to work for the fur trade in Canada, they brought with them many of their customs, including Scottish fiddle music. French fur traders also shared their fiddle music. These styles of fiddling were adopted by the Métis, and Métis fiddle playing evolved into its own unique style. European-made fiddles were not easily obtained in Canada, so fiddles were constructed by Métis artisans with maple and birch wood.

Jigging is a type of dance that was introduced to the Métis by Europeans, who brought their traditional step dancing to Canada. Métis children learned and changed the dances to suit Métis fiddle music. The Red River jig is one dance that developed as a result.

Métis fiddles were traditionally accompanied by the tapping of heels, spoons, or tin pans. Today, Metis musicians play many other instruments, including guitars.

The Red River jig gives dancers a chance to compete against one another as each tries to perform the most impressive fancy dance steps. Jigging is hard work and fast paced. Thick-heeled shoes pound out rhythms in time with the music. A dancer's heels provide a form of **percussion** for the Métis fiddle music. Traditionally, the dance has four sets of partners dancing a quick step while forming circles, squares, and lines—all to a bouncing beat. Women dancers wear colourful skirts and blouses, and the men wear shirts stitched with ribbons or beadwork. A sash is another important piece of clothing worn during the dance.

The Métis fiddle is tuned differently than other types of fiddle. This unique tuning creates a faster beat, making it perfect for jigging.

Language and Storytelling

Today, many Métis people speak an Aboriginal language, such as Cree or Saulteaux. The Métis even created their own language called Michif. As with so many other parts of traditional Métis culture, Michif was created from a blend of First Nations and European words. Michif includes languages such as Plains or Woodland Cree, Ojibwa, Saulteaux, English, and French.

The Aboriginal tradition of teaching through stories was often part of Métis children's education. Grandmothers or grandfathers would gather children by the fireplace or around a campfire at night to tell stories. The stories were a bridge between the children's First Nations heritage and their Métis community. They were an important teaching tool and often included valuable lessons about life for both children and adults.

The Niwasa Head Start Preschool in Hamilton, Ontario, is just one program that teaches First Nations languages to its Aboriginal students.

MICHIF

One of the most important characters in Métis stories is Wisahkechak. Storytellers taught lessons through the adventures of Wisahkechak. These lessons included important Aboriginal spiritual beliefs about respecting the natural world and other people.

Storytellers would sometimes compete with each other to see who could tell the most interesting tale. Scary stories are fun and thrilling, so these were told to children to help teach them about the dangers of the natural world. A black dog or wolf would appear in a story as a warning that characters in a story should take care and watch out for danger.

In Métis stories, the black dog often appears unexpectedly.

Some Michif words come from the French language, but have been adapted to suit Cree pronunciations.

English	French	Michif
One	Un	Haen
Two	Deux	Deu
Three	Trois	Trwaw
Four	Quatre	Kaet
Five	Cinq	Saenk
Dog	Chien	Sh'yaen
Sun	Soleil	Salay
White	Blanc	Blawn
Yellow	Jaune	Zhounn
Red	Rouge	Roozh
Black	Noir	Nwayr

Métis Art

The beadwork on Métis clothing is so colourful and detailed that it has become an art form. Métis women use small glass beads called seed beads. These beads were introduced to Aboriginal Peoples by Europeans and were quickly adopted into Aboriginal art. In the past, the Métis were easily recognized by the pretty flowers and green winding vines adorning their clothes. Métis items adorned with floral patterns were traded and made their way across the country with fur traders.

Métis beadwork was greatly influenced by **embroidery** patterns. Prior to European contact, Aboriginal women had stitched with porcupine quills and used plants to create colour on garments. When **nuns** from France came to North America, they showed Métis women how to stitch fancy embroidery. The Métis used embroidery on most of their cloth items, including clothing, tablecloths, pillow cases, picture frames, and religious decorations.

After the arrival of European nuns, many Métis continued to use traditional materials such as porcupine quills, to decorate items using these new patterns.

As the fur trade slowed down and there were fewer furs to sell, Métis women sold their embroidered creations. Beaded items such as purses or slippers were sold across North America. Métis artists today borrow from the flower designs to create art with paints or clay.

Today, many Métis artists make a living selling their artwork, including embroidered clothing.

Traditional European embroidery is made by stitching dyed threads onto a velvet or hide base in a variety of designs. Métis women used these materials, along with others, for their embroidery. White **guard hairs** from moose or caribou were one material that could be tufted into a pattern. These hairs were dyed in the same fashion as thread. The hair was not long enough to be sewn into the hide, so it was gathered in bunches and placed into an outline of the pattern, where it was secured into place by sinew or cotton thread. Another way to embroider with guard hairs was to wrap the hair with thread and place it on the pattern in thin lines.

The Métis Flag

The Métis in Canada have their own flag. The flag has either a red or blue background and a white circle eight, or infinity symbol, in the center. The Métis flag is flown by different Métis groups across Canada. The two circles joined together represent the merging of the two distinct heritages that created the Métis people.

The Métis flag was created early in the history of the country. In fact, it is the oldest patriotic flag **indigenous** to Canada. The Métis flag is more than 150 years older than Canada's maple leaf flag. The flag flies today as a source of Métis pride.

The colours of the Métis flag are believed to represent parts of Métis history. The blue is said to represent the North West Company from the fur-trade era, while red was the colour used to represent the Hudson's Bay Company.

MODERN ARTIST

Christi Belcourt

Christi Belcourt is a Métis artist who expresses the art of traditional embroidery and beadwork in her paintings. Drops of paint are placed on canvas to look like beads. Hundreds of these drops become patterns that resemble the designs of Métis embroidery. All of these designs are raised drops of paint. This allows the viewer to also feel the painting. Christi calls this "touching the past." She believes it can help people make connections between the past and present.

The flowers and plants that Christi uses in her paintings are beautiful floral designs, but they also represent how she sees the world. Christi's painted flowers represent the Métis people. Roots of these flowers are included in some of her paintings to show how Métis people are supported and encouraged by their heritage.

As a well-known and respected Métis artist, Christi has won many awards. She has received awards from the Canada Council for the Arts, the Ontario Arts Council, and the Métis Nation of Ontario. Christi lives near the LaCloche mountain range near Manitoulin Island in Ontario. The mountain flowers and plants inspire Christie's paintings. Some of her paintings are on permanent display in art galleries across Canada.

Christi Belcourt's art reflects her belief in the interconnectedness of all things.

Studying the Past

Archaeologists learn about the Métis' past by locating and studying the things that they have left behind. Old buildings, abandoned boats, or even buried garbage all tell archaeologists how the Métis lived. Where the objects are found also tells a story of where the Métis lived and how long they stayed in that area.

Written historical records help archaeologists learn about the Métis. These records, such as journals written by fur traders, provide details of Métis life in the past. Stories passed from generation to generation also describe the history of the Métis. Archaeologists gather these pieces of information to create a picture of the Métis' way of life and their work.

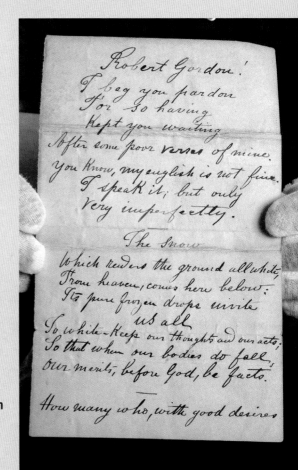

A poem written by Louis Riel, three weeks before his death, is a very important item in Métis history. The poem helps explain Riel's feelings towards the Canadian government during the Northwest Resistance.

Contact Period
AD 1000-1600

Explorers from France arrive on the eastern coast of Canada. Aboriginal Peoples welcome and trade with the newcomers. The tradition of marrying to create strong family and trade ties encourages marriages between Aboriginal women and European men.

Early Fur Trade
1600-1800

Fur-trade companies set up forts and posts along the shores of the Great Lakes and Hudson Bay. The trade slowly moves farther west along river transport systems. The Métis work for the fur-trade companies and live near the forts.

Settlement
1800-1850

The Battle of Seven Oaks in 1816 is the first time the Métis take a stand against unfair treatment by the Canadian government. The Métis flag is created, and the Métis begin to shape their unique identity within Canada.

Resistance
1850-1900

The Hudson's Bay Company gives the land now known as western Canada to the Canadian government. The Métis are afraid they will lose their rights and land claims, so they form a **provisional** government. Louis Riel is asked by the Métis to lead this new government. Battles are fought between the Métis and the Government of Canada in 1869 at Red River in Manitoba, and again in 1885 at Batoche, Saskatchewan. The Métis lose the Battle of Batoche. Louis Riel is captured and hanged for treason on November 16, 1885.

Present
1900-Today

In 1982, the Canadian government writes a new constitution in which the Métis are recognized as a distinct people. The Métis National Council is formed to represent the Métis on a national basis.

Louis Riel is also known as the founder of Manitoba.

Métis Tufting

Métis women created embroidered designs with moose or caribou guard hairs. Try using this method to create floral patterns of your own.

Materials

construction paper	dry paint
white pencil crayon	glue
cotton balls	

1. Take a black piece of construction paper and a white pencil crayon. Use the pencil to make dots and create shapes of flowers, stems, and leaves.

2. Put the dried paint in small separate bowls.

3. Dip cotton balls into the dried paint until they are covered with colour.

4. Glue the cotton balls inside the design pattern.

5. A beautiful picture will slowly be revealed as each of the coloured cotton balls are glued into place.

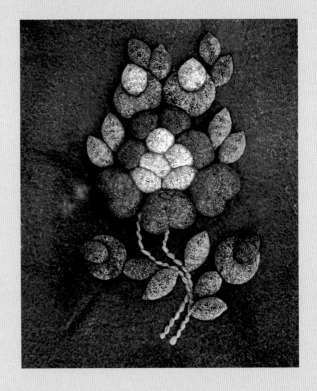

Further Reading

To learn more about Métis culture, read *The Métis in Canada* by Heather C. Hudak (Weigl Educational Publishers Limited, 2006). This book shows how the Métis are a unique and integral part of Canada.

Take a journey to the Moon with Wisahkechak in *Wisahkechak Flies to the Moon* by Freda Ahenakew (Pemmican Publications, 2001), and learn an important Métis lesson.

Websites

The history of the Métis is explored at the Library and Archives of Canada website. **www.lac-bac.gc.ca/settlement /kids/021013-2081-e.html**

View some of Christi Belcourt's artwork at **www.belcourt.net**.

Canada's Museum of Civilization describes Métis bison hunting techniques at **www.civilization.ca/hist/ canp1/ca13eng.html**.

GLOSSARY

INDEX

Aboriginal Peoples: original inhabitants of a country

ancestors: relatives who lived a long time ago

archaeologists: scientists who study objects from the past to learn about people who lived long ago

Christian: related to Christianity, a religion based upon the life and teachings of Jesus Christ

economical: thrifty

elders: the older and more influential members of a community

embroidery: patterns made on cloth using a needle and thread

factor: the top person who worked at a fur-trade company fort

First Nations: members of Canada's Aboriginal community who are not Inuit or Métis

fur trade: the exchange of furs for European goods

guard hairs: the white hairs from the neck of a moose or caribou

heritage: the people, places, and culture of the past

indigenous: originating in a certain country or region

missions: places where people teach others about their religion

moccasins: shoes crafted by Aboriginal or Métis people that are made from hides and are suited to the Canadian climate

Northwest Resistance: an uprising of Métis and First Nations peoples in Saskatchewan in 1885

nuns: women who are committed to and work for the church

percussion: the part of music that contains the beat

point blankets: blankets used as money by the Hudson's Bay Company during the fur trade

powwow: an Aboriginal Peoples' gathering and celebration

provisional: temporary

spiritual: sacred or religious

teepees: structures made up of 12 or more long poles set upright in a circle with hides or canvas stretched over top

traditional: based on the ways of others who lived before

treason: the act of betraying one's country

voyageur: a canoeman who worked for fur-trade companies